"Thanks to Omega-3s, I can live a more active and healthy life."

Gary C.
Laureldale, PA

When I was 39, I began an exercise routine. Five years into running and working out, my mother died from heart disease. My father died from a series of strokes. As I approached 60, I began to think about my parents and their heart problems. Along with exercise, I began using vitamins and supplements such as Omega-3. Since doing so, my annual checkups are great.

I have as much energy to race in triathlons now as I did when I was 45. Now at 64, I can't wait 'til summer for the next season. I believe Omega-3s keep my arteries open and blood flowing to vital organs and limbs. My endurance has also remained very high. Since turning 60, I have placed in the top three in my age group in every race – a total of 19 awards in the past four years.

Learning about my possible inherited health problems helped me make healthier choices. Thanks to research and supplements like Omega-3, I can live a more active and healthy life.

"I will always take Omega-3s..."

I started taking Omega-3s in 1997 – weight gain, asthma, and mood problems were some of the symptoms I was having. After taking Omega-3s, I lost weight and my hair and nails and skin improved – I felt great! I will always take Omega-3s – they are recommended by the Mayo Clinic Newsletter I subscribe to, as well as the Harvard Health Newsletter.

Harriet G.
Mahwah, NJ

The information presented in this booklet is based upon research and personal and professional experiences of the authors and consumers. This book is not intended as a substitute for consulting with your physician or other licensed healthcare practitioners. This booklet does not provide medical advice or attempt to diagnose or treat an illness which should be done under the direction of a healthcare professional.

The publisher and authors are not responsible for any adverse effects or consequences resulting from the use of the suggestions, preparations, or procedures discussed in this book. Should the reader have any questions concerning the appropriateness of any procedures or preparation mentioned, the authors and the publisher strongly suggest consulting a professional healthcare advisor.

The testimonials, consumer letters and quotes by third parties were obtained by the publisher as a result of a contest. Some of the consumers whose testimonials appear in this book were awarded prizes. All testimonials, consumer letters and quotes by third parties used in this book are their own experiences and have not been edited or revised except for grammatical and space considerations. In some testimonial consumer letters, specific product name mentions were replaced with those products' main nutritional ingredients. All consumer letters, quotes and likenesses are reprinted with permission.

Vibrant Life Publishing, Inc.
1427 E. Hillsboro Blvd.
Suite 425
Deerfield Beach, Florida 33441
www.vibrantlifepublishing.com

Copyright© 2008 by Vibrant Life Publishing, Inc.

ISBN: 978-0-9815547-1-6

Printed in the USA

TABLE OF CONTENTS

INTRO: Michael Ozner, MD, FACC, FAHA......................Page 4

CHAPTER 1:   Your Ultimate Desert Island Nutrients
Omega-3s are true multi-taskers........................Page 5

CHAPTER 2:   Starting Life Right
The Miracle of Life depends on Omega-3s........ Page 9

CHAPTER 3:   Thinking Clearly at Any Age
Omega-3s and peak cognitive function.............. Page 13

CHAPTER 4:   Scientific Support for a Healthy Heart
Omega-3s' cardiovascular claim to fame............Page 15

CHAPTER 5:   Proper Immune Response
An Omega-3 connection.................................... Page 19

CHAPTER 6:   Health Benefits You Never Imagined
Omega 3s' surprising secrets...........................Page 23

CHAPTER 7:   Nature's Gift for Vibrant Life
Feeling great with Omega-3s............................ Page 28

REFERENCES.. Page 31

By Michael Ozner, MD, FACC, FAHA

Despite our modern world's advancements, it is the most ancient of diets – featuring simple, unrefined whole foods – that may hold the secret to true well-being. The Mediterranean Diet is one such traditional way of eating that offers amazing benefits for health and vitality. Known for its fresh fruits and vegetables, whole grains, nuts, fish, olive oil and red wine (in moderation), the Mediterranean Diet provides a health-promoting nutritional profile of anti-oxidants, fiber, phytonutrients and good fats. Omega-3 fatty acids – found most abundantly in oily fish, but also in flax, walnuts and some vegetables – are one of the reasons why cultures that favor the Mediterranean Diet enjoy such long, energetic and healthy lives.

Have you ever wondered why fish is "brain food?" Omega-3s found in fish help to form brain cells and keep them functioning properly, yielding impressive benefits for memory, mood and peak cognitive function. Omega-3s are also natural anti-inflammatories, fighting heart disease, inflammatory bowel disease, arthritis and many other conditions associated with chronic inflammation. Omega-3s' critical role in cell formation and performance unlocks even more remarkable benefits across diverse body systems, helping with asthma, weight loss, migraines and more.

When it comes to health, Omega-3s are Nature's nutritional masterpieces. From promoting fetal development to ensuring peak mobility and mental clarity in later years, no other family of nutrients can match Omega-3s' life-enhancing benefits. It is no coincidence that Omega-3s just happen to be found in the Mediterranean Diet's fish and other staple foods. Nature, in all her wisdom, placed Omega-3s and other important nutrients in delicious, satisfying foods we can easily incorporate into our diets. These simple dietary changes can help us work in harmony with Nature – so we can enjoy the healthy, exhilarating lives we are all meant to be living.

Michael Ozner, MD, FACC, FAHA is one of America's leading advocates for heart disease prevention and a well-known speaker in the field of preventive cardiology. Dr. Ozner is a board certified cardiologist, a Fellow of the American College of Cardiology and American Heart Association, and medical director of the Center for Wellness & Prevention at Baptist Health South Florida and Cardiovascular Prevention Institute of South Florida. Dr. Ozner is author of "The Miami Mediterranean Diet" (Benbella Books) and the forthcoming book "The Great American Heart Hoax" (Benbella Books, December 2008). Dr. Ozner's website is www.drozner.com.

Your Ultimate Desert Island Nutrients

I started taking Omega-3s approximately four years ago. At the time I was 60 years of age and went on a very intense search for supplements to maintain my energy, health and skin. My doctor suggested Omega-3s, so I proceeded to do research on them. I fell in love with Omega-3s... they have improved my life completely! My skin is fantastic and my energy level is unbelievable... I call Omega-3 my very own "MIRACLE SUPPLEMENT." Everyone tells me that I do not look my age. I put my husband on Omega-3s and he too has blossomed.

I feel like Omega-3s are the secret to prolonged health and vitality. I watched my husband's blood pressure go down tremendously; the doctor was amazed. I love the effects! My weight is perfect, skin, and overall

health is wonderful. I'm a big believer that one does not have to give in to age – anyone, and I mean anyone, can look great, feel great, and experience a much fuller life by just taking the proper supplements. I attribute my incredible outlook on life and energy to Omega-3s. I feel so very blessed to have the opportunity to experience such a dynamic life at age 64... I can't express to you how very much my whole life has improved in every aspect with this wonder supplement.

Marleen M.
Rancho Cucamonga, CA

If you were stranded on a desert island and were granted an unlimited supply of one nutritional supplement, what would it be? You would probably choose a "multi-tasker" supplement; one that helps your health and well-being in a number of different ways.

Even if your desert island doesn't come equipped with a health food store, you might still have access to the ultimate "multi-tasker" nutrients – as long

as you can catch fish. Omega-3 fatty acids, most famously found in fish oils, are a family of nutrients that provide an amazing array of health benefits across numerous body systems. Hundreds of studies have investigated Omega-3s' potential health benefits in the following areas, to name a few:

- Heart Health
- Brain Health
- Blood Pressure
- Inflammation Modulation
- Immune Function
- Migraines
- PMS
- Weight Management Support
- Skin, Hair & Nail Health
- Peak Energy
- Joint Health
- Eye Health

Omega-3s' multifaceted positive impact on overall well-being is evident in the true stories featured throughout this book… you'll have a hard time finding a story that discusses only one Omega-3 health benefit!

WHAT'S AN OMEGA-3 FATTY ACID?

By now, it's common knowledge: not all fats are bad. In fact, Omega-3 fatty acids are considered to be the "good fats" which help to balance the "bad fats" in your diet. The Omega-3 fatty acids include **alpha-linolenic acid** (ALA), **eicosapentaenoic acid** (EPA) and **docosahexaenoic acid** (DHA). Many experts place these Omegas under the umbrella of "Essential Fatty Acids" (EFAs), meaning that they must be obtained from the diet. So why are Omega-3s so important to health? Many of Omega-3s' beneficial activities can be traced back to two health-supporting functions within the body:

OMEGA-3 FUNCTION 1:
PROMOTING HEALTHY CELL MEMBRANES

There are trillions upon trillions of cells in the human body. In each and every one, fatty acids form cell membranes. Hardly static barriers, cell membranes are actively involved in a number of sophisticated tasks, including hormone and immune responses, cellular nutrition intake, waste disposal, and cellular communication.

We are what we eat – especially when it comes to our cells. When the body creates cell membranes, it uses whatever fatty acids are available. Consuming excessive saturated fats (or even worse, dreaded trans-fats) can make cell membranes stiff and unhealthy,[1] lacking the fluidity needed to best perform vital functions.

Unsaturated fats like Omega-3s, however, are excellent building materials – enabling the body to create cell membranes that are healthy and fluid,[2] like fish oil or olive oil at room temperature. Supple, flexible cell membranes formed with Omega-3s are believed to benefit cell functions.[3,4] As a result, Omega-3 fatty acids are considered some of the most important fatty acids you need for cellular health. They are essential for normal cell growth, play a key structural role in cell membranes, and help to regulate electrolyte transport, hormone and immune responses, and cell fluidity. As Omega-3s promote cellular health, we get a hint of just how truly amazing and important these nutrients are.

OMEGA-3 FUNCTION 2:
PRODUCTION OF EICOSANOIDS

Enzymes release fatty acids from cell membranes to create hormone-like substances called "eicosanoids" (eye-KOE-zuh-noids) that regulate a myriad of important body functions, including cell growth, inflammation, blood clotting, nerve transmission, blood pressure, circulation, muscle function and more.[5]

Different fatty acids make eicosanoids that regulate functions with different signals. Certain Omega-6 fatty acids, for example, are associated with aggressive, inflammatory signaling reactions. Such reactions are necessary at times; if you were bleeding from a serious cut, an aggressive signal would enable blood to clot and stop the bleeding.

Enzymes use Omega-3s, on the other hand, to make "good" eicosanoids that help keep aggressive signals from spinning out of control and causing health problems. For example, Omega-3 eicosanoids respond to injury or infection with gentle signals that modulate inflammation – as a result, the body reacts appropriately instead of overreacting.[6]

THE PROBLEM:
WHAT'S YOUR RATIO?

The body needs Omega-6 and Omega-3 fatty acids – but for peak well-being, these essential nutrients must be consumed in the right proportions. Some experts believe that a 1:1 ratio of Omega-6 to Omega-3 fatty acids is best for balanced eicosanoid performance. Unfortunately, the average American diet is estimated at a 20:1 ratio. Experts believe that this wildly unbalanced ratio may be the reason behind escalating chronic disease in America.[7] Check the following chart of dietary essential fatty acid sources – considering how often you consume these foods, what's *your* omega ratio?

Omega-6 Foods	Omega-3 Foods
Most fried foods	Fish (and fish oil)
Bread	Soybeans
Most processed foods	Walnuts
Beef (grain fed)	Flaxseed (and flaxseed oil)
Chicken	Chia seed
Eggs	Kiwis
Most vegetable oils	Grass-fed beef & dairy
Cereals	Olive oil
Cheese & dairy (grain fed)	Leafy green vegetables

Did you know?
Overly aggressive eicosanoid signaling may hurt your health. **Excessive Omega-6 eicosanoids are associated with heart attacks, headaches, PMS, arthritis, chronic inflammation, osteoporosis, mood disorders and cancer.**[8] Omega-3s help to balance these harmful signals.

Balancing your omega ratio can be challenging – as the chart at right illustrates, Americans fall far short of recommended levels of the Omega-3s ALA, EPA and DHA. Complicating matters, Omega-3s are fragile and can be lost in cooking or processing.[9] Even consuming more fish is not a surefire solution; many commercially-available fish are farm-raised, which may have lower levels of Omega-3s and may contain PCBs, chemicals that can have serious long-term health implications.[10]

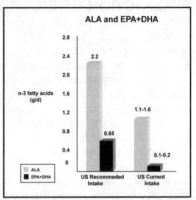

Source: Kris-Etherton et al. PUFAs In the Food Chain: United States.
Am J Clin Nutr., Volume 71, Issue 1, p.179S-188S (2000)

Did you know?
According to the Third National Health and Nutrition Examination, only 25% of Americans reported any daily intake of the Omega-3s EPA or DHA.[11]

Are you among the millions of Americans who may be Omega-3 deficient? According to the University of Maryland Medical Center and other sources, the following symptoms are associated with Omega-3 deficiency:[12, 13]

- Fatigue
- Unhealthy Skin, Hair and Nails
- Mood Swings
- Frequent Colds
- Poor Concentration and Memory
- Joint Discomfort

A SUPPLEMENT SOLUTION:
To achieve Omega-3s' health benefits, many are taking supplements in addition to consuming Omega-3 foods. Supplements offer special advantages:

• **Omega-3 supplements deliver precise levels of Omega-3s.**
• **Omega-3 supplements can be tested for purity, potency and safety.**
• **Omega-3 supplements are accessible, affordable and convenient.**

Your friends, family and neighbors are taking control of their health destiny by consuming Omega-3 foods and taking Omega-3 supplements. Fish oil supplement sales are skyrocketing as a result, and all signs say this red-hot health trend is here to stay. Let's now examine the scientific evidence behind Omega-3s' rise to fame – and discover exactly what Omega-3s can do.

Starting Life Right

"I have my life back, and I am eternally grateful."

I began taking Omega-3s on a recommendation made by my naturopath. Despite being fairly young, I had been experiencing a plethora of health problems including asthma, insomnia, elevated blood pressure and memory loss since the birth of my child several months prior. My weight had returned to normal; my breathing and sleeping patterns, however, had not. I couldn't walk up a single flight of stairs without experiencing shortness of breath. My health was interfering with my ability to care for my little one.

Within two weeks of starting the Omega-3s, I began to notice that I could carry the baby upstairs without becoming winded. I observed small changes in my ability to concentrate; I was able to stay on task and did not find my mind wandering as I had in weeks past. My suspicions were confirmed when I went in for a checkup with my doctor and found my blood pressure within normal range for the first time since giving birth. I have my life back, and I am eternally grateful.

**Stella I.
Portsmouth, OH**

"Omega oils are 'Liquid Gold.'"

Several years ago, my daughter Amanda (age 8) was having a difficult time in her second grade class. She was unable to focus on lessons, concentrate on her work, or sit for long periods of time. Her teachers were finding her behavior disruptive. She also experienced mood swings and frequently had sudden outbursts. I made appointments with counselors and eventually Amanda was speaking to a counselor on a regular basis. I had accepted that we were all on a long journey of raising a strong-willed and emotionally explosive child.

One day I was reading a nutritional article about Omega fatty acids and the lack of these essential nutrients in our foods. The article described how essential fatty acids can help support a person's mood and cognitive behavior. At the time I was somewhat skeptical, but I decided it was worth trying. The next day I was in the local nutrition store purchasing fish oil and flax oil.

I began with small doses for my daughter mixed in juice or yogurt. Within days we were noticing a remarkable change. Within a week I was receiving notes from her teacher describing Amanda's behavior to be exemplary.

Nicole C.
Yorktown, VA

Her mood swings decreased and she was concentrating better. Even her handwriting became neater. The changes were dramatic.

Today at 12 years of age Amanda takes flax oil and fish oil every day. Amanda notices when she misses one day of her oils. For several years everyone in our family, including my parents, have benefited from taking Omegas on a regular basis. We have experienced benefits with our blood pressure, heart health, mood and cognition. This is why my family refers to the Omega oils as "Liquid Gold."

MIRACLE OF LIFE

Prenatal development and birth are truly miraculous. From the embryonic to fetal period, a staggering number of complex processes are all in motion, gradually transforming a tiny embryo into a thriving infant. Among the most beneficial nutrients presented by nature during these key months are Omega-3s, which are crucial to life from the moment it begins. Many well-designed studies suggest that Omega-3s are among the most important pregnancy nutrients – for both mother and child.

DURING PREGNANCY:

While a baby is still in the womb, Omega-3s are essential for healthy eye, brain, and nervous system development. Studies have shown that the retina and occipital cortex both benefit from increased levels of DHA, as does the central nervous system.[14]

- In one study, researchers focused on the Inuit people in Northern Quebec – a group that subsists on a heavy diet of Omega-3-rich fish. They found that a higher concentration of DHA in the umbilical cord of Inuit infants is associated with better visual, cognitive, and motor development, pointing to the importance of Omega-3s, particularly during the final trimester of pregnancy.[15] Around this time, these fatty acids, most notably DHA, collect in the brain and eyes of a fetus, becoming building blocks that prepare the baby for its entry into the world.[16]

During the course of pregnancy, women without adequate Omega-3s may be more susceptible to complications.

- A study on women in early pregnancy revealed that low seafood consumption was linked to greater risk of both preterm labor and low birth weight. While the group that never consumed fish had a 7.1% occurrence of preterm delivery, the group that ate fish at least once per week had only a 1.9% occurrence of preterm delivery.[17]
- Research has also shown that Omega-3s may protect against preeclampsia (pregnancy-induced hypertension) by performing a number of biochemical roles, including supporting healthy blood pressure.[18]

Did you know?
Although seafood is one of the main sources of Omega-3s, mercury levels found in some fish can pose a health risk to developing babies. As an alternative to consuming fish, expecting and new mothers can seek out Omega-3 supplements that have been certified "mercury-free."

AFTER PREGNANCY

Omega-3s may continue helping mothers even after they give birth. After delivery, mothers tend to experience a notable loss of Omega-3s due to both the strain of delivery and lactation, in which Omega-3s are transferred to the baby via breast milk. This reduction of Omega-3s may play a role in post-partum mood problems.[19] Research suggests that Omega-3s may help to support a brighter outlook for new mothers:

- One Omega-3 study found that countries with high consumption of fish (such as Japan and Sweden) had low rates of post-partum mood problems, while countries with low fish consumption (including South Africa and West Germany) had some of the highest global levels of post-partum mood problems.[20]

Did you know?
Since DHA is an important nutritional component of breast milk, supplemental DHA is especially important for mothers who can't nurse. DHA is often paired in a healthy ratio with arachidonic acid (ARA), an Omega-6 fatty acid, and added to infant formula in order to create a mixture that attempts to emulate the beneficial nutrition found in breast milk. Such supplement formulas were approved by the Food and Drug Administration (FDA) in 2001.

EARLY CHILDHOOD AND BEYOND

Omega-3s' support for healthy cognitive development starts in the womb and continues after an infant enters the world. Indeed, it appears that Omega-3s play an important role in promoting healthy development of faculties that would help enable a child to excel at academics, coordination[21] and socialization — supporting a vibrant youth that every child deserves!

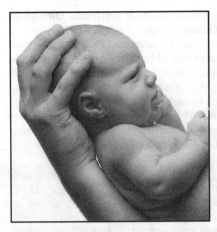

Omega-3s may support healthy nerves and vision. Retinopathy of prematurity (ROP) is an eye disease that affects preterm infants, particularly those who continue to have an inadequate supply of Omega-3s after birth. Researchers have found that Omega-3 intake in premature babies may significantly decrease the occurrence of ROP.[22] Since Omega-3s also assist in building the body's nervous system, a notable lack of these fatty acids may hinder nerve development in the same way that it affects optic development.

Studies suggest that infants who receive significant Omega-3s from their mothers in the womb, after they are born, and into early childhood have exhibited higher intelligence. As children grow, Omega-3s appear to help support focus and general academic performance.[23]

- In one placebo-controlled study, women took 1,183 mg of the Omega-3 DHA (in the form of cod liver oil) beginning at the 18th week of pregnancy and ending three months after delivery. All babies in the study were breast fed, and then took intelligence tests at age four. The children whose mothers took DHA scored significantly higher on mental processing than the children whose mothers took the placebo – leading researchers to conclude that mothers' intake of Omega-3 fatty acids during pregnancy and while nursing may be favorable for later mental development of children.[24]

Omega-3 deficiency in children has been linked to behavioral problems. Research has pointed to a greater number of behavioral difficulties – including poor focus in learning, temper tantrums and sleep problems – in boys with lower levels of Omega-3s in their blood plasma.[25]

Performing such integral roles in healthy pregnancy and early development, Omega-3s appear to be intertwined with our very survival as a species through the ages. One can't help but to marvel at nature's sublime design; hiding these nutrients for humanity in the fish and flax that would become staples of ancient diets.

Read on to learn about how Omega-3s help us to not only grow, but prosper – by promoting the satisfying existence that is synonymous with peak brain health.

Thinking Clearly at any Age

> *"We have both noticed a marked improvement in memory and mood."*

We started taking Omega-3s as a supplement several years ago as an aid to improving memory and mood. Prior to that time we noticed some forgetfulness and mood swings that we were uncomfortable with. Since taking Omega-3s regularly, we have both noticed a marked improvement in memory and mood. We are now aged 75 and 78. We have good health and feel good and walk two and a half miles every day. I have also lost some weight!

Lowell & Beverly D.
Fortuna, CA

> *"In less than two weeks I was feeling better..."*

Dan W.
Enterprise, OR

As I approached 50 years of age, I was increasingly unhappy. I felt stuck in a life that I had not imagined... every day was just another day to get through somehow. I exercised regularly and had a fairly healthy diet, but I could just not generate any happiness or optimism.

My wife researched on the web and discovered that Omega-3 fatty acids were one of the things that were recommended to help with mood problems. I ordered flax seed oil [rich in Omega-3s] and started taking it in the morning and again in the evening. In less than two weeks I was feeling better. I have continued to take this supplement and continue to enjoy feeling good. I still don't like getting old, but at least I am happy while doing so.

A Brainy Species

Humans are far from the most physically formidable creatures on the planet. We're not the fastest; we're not the strongest; and we certainly don't have the endurance of many other mammals. What we do have, however, is highly developed brains... but how did we gain that advantage? Dr. Barry Sears, in his book *The Omega Rx Zone* (Collins), theorizes that humans evolved in coastal areas because the Omega-3 fatty acids found in fish were necessary for our accelerated brain development.

Omega-3s also provide nutritional support for our brains throughout our lives – helping to ensure healthy development, sharp cognitive performance, detailed memory and crystalline mental clarity well into our later decades. With these far-ranging benefits, Omega-3s can be viewed as our nutritional foundation for intelligence, mental and emotional stability, personal success, and overall quality of life.

Omega-3s can assist in shaping a healthy adulthood, from 25 to 45 to 65 and beyond, allowing for better cognitive aging throughout the decades. Specific benefits may vary, but many of them seem to stem from Omega-3s' ability to keep the brain's all-important neurons finely tuned, assuring open lines of communication as information is received and transmitted.[26]

Studies suggest that Omega-3s may assist in maintaining a positive mood.

- Researchers monitoring a group of healthy adult volunteers noted that participants with higher blood levels of Omega-3s tended to have brighter outlooks on life, while those with lower levels were more impulsive and pessimistic.[27] In fact, another study points to a lack of Omega-3s as being a marker for two prominent mood disorders.[28]

Omega-3s have been linked to increased concentration and memory, allowing for better focus and information retention. Studies note that this appears to be due to Omega-3s' positive effects on synaptic transmission, which goes hand in hand with benefiting the central nervous system.[29]

Middle-aged people with regular intake of Omega-3s tend to have a reduced risk of impaired cognitive function.[30] Moving into the golden years, Omega-3s, particularly DHA, have been associated with reduced incidence of memory impairment.[31]

- A study found that elderly people who ate fish or seafood regularly (once a week) had a distinctly reduced risk of developing memory impairment. Researchers concluded that fish's Omega-3s may help keep memory sharp by modulating brain inflammation and helping to regenerate neurons.[32]

With such evidence, it's clear that Omega-3s may be part of the lifestyle that helps us maintain the brain health that is so crucial to quality of life. But we can only enjoy this vibrant existence by staying alive – and as it turns out, Omega-3s may help promote longevity by helping to fight the most dangerous killer we know: heart disease.

Scientific Support For a Healthy Heart

In late October 2005, I had a close call with death at age 63 while undergoing two separate heart bypass surgeries; the second operation corrected a life-threatening graft collapse and heart arrhythmia that occurred in the ICU after the first surgery. Prior to this, I had a quadruple bypass in 1995. So, while recovering at home, I decided that I would do my best to avoid another bypass operation and do what I could to live a healthy life free from burning chest discomfort, ambulance trips to hospitals, and fear.

**Thomas D.
Battle Creek, MI**

I began studying information about nutritional supplements and heart health. One afternoon, I was watching a TV interview with a noted cardiac nutritionist who stated that if he were forced to select one supplement for heart health, it would be fish oil with its Omega-3 fatty acids. Thus, I started taking a fish oil supplement. Since beginning this regimen, I have noticed improved blood pressure, increased mental and physical vigor, and feelings of peace, confidence and well-being. I am very glad that I discovered the Omega-3 fatty acids that have positively impacted my life.

It was January 6, 2008, and I was departing from church when my life suddenly flashed before my eyes. My car had surged across a busy intersection. Surrounded by a crowd of strangers and taken to the hospital, I was later notified that I had collapsed in my car while driving. I was diagnosed with cholesterol of 280 and Mitral valve prolapse with a leaking valve. I was informed by the physician that I needed valve repair. Previously, I had been experiencing shortness of breath, dizziness, hypotension and palpitations. Approximately two months ago, I began taking fish oil (Omega-3s, DHA & EPA) – and my cholesterol has already dropped to 240.

**Sonya J.
Merrillville, IN**

Public Enemy #1

According to the National Vital Statistics Report released in April of 2008, heart disease was the biggest killer in America, responsible for over 650,000 deaths in 2005 – that's over 25% of all deaths.[33] In May of 2008, The World Health Organization (WHO) released its World Health Statistics 2008 report, which revealed that heart disease is not just the leading cause of death in America, but is also the most formidable killer in the world – killing 17.1 million worldwide in 2007, with that number projected to swell to 23.4 million by 2030.[34]

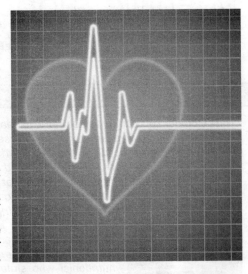

Of all Omega-3s' beneficial activities, none is more proven than their ability to support heart health. The past decade has seen Omega-3s rise to prominence in the heart health arena:

- **2002**: The American Heart Association recommended that healthy adults consume two servings of fish a week, especially varieties of fish that are rich in the Omega-3s EPA and DHA. Additionally, the American Heart Association suggested that those at higher risk of cardiovascular disease consume more EPA and DHA, and should consider taking an omega-3 supplement under a physician's direction.[35]
- **2002**: The National Academy of Sciences (recognized as the highest scientific body in the U.S.) recommended that men consume 1.6 grams and women consume 1.1 grams of Omega-3s each day – noting that the Omega-3s may afford some protection against coronary heart disease.[36]
- **2004**: The FDA allowed a qualified health claim for reduced risk of coronary heart disease. The claim states: "Supportive but not conclusive research shows that consumption of EPA and DHA omega-3 fatty acids may reduce the risk of coronary heart disease. One serving of [name of food] provides [x] grams of EPA and DHA omega-3 fatty acids."[37]
- **2005**: The Dietary Guidelines Advisory Committee released its recommendation suggesting consumption of two 4-ounce servings of fish high in EPA and DHA per week to reduce the risk of coronary heart disease.[38]

Health experts and respected health organizations are increasingly in agreement: Omega-3s may offer significant nutritional support for the

heart and cardiovascular system. But how exactly do Omega-3s do it? Research suggests that Omega-3s – staying true to their "multi-tasker" form – help to promote cardiovascular health through a variety of actions:

- **Omega-3s help to support healthy, stable heart rhythm.**[39] Arrythmias are a primary precursor to sudden cardiac death.
- **Omega-3s help to modulate inflammatory response;**[40] inflammation is one of the key markers in predicting coronary events.
- **Omega-3s help to relax the arteries and help to maintain arteries' flexibility or "elasticity."**[41, 42] Narrowing and hardening of arteries, also known as atherosclerosis, is a risk factor for cardiovascular disease.
- **Omega 3s help to support healthy circulation and maintain cardio-vascular system health.**[43] One aspect of this support appears to involve Omega 3s' inhibition of thromboxane A2, an eicosanoid that is linked with artery constriction and the platelet clumping that precedes blood clots.[44]
- **Omega 3s help to keep triglycerides (a type of blood fat) and very low-density lipoprotein (LDL, also known as bad cholesterol) in a healthy range.**[45] Triglycerides and LDL are considered major risk factors for heart disease when elevated in the blood.
- **Omega 3s may help to support healthy blood pressure.**[46, 47] High blood pressure increases risk for heart attack and stroke.

Stable heart rhythm, appropriate inflammatory response, flexible and relaxed arteries, healthy circulation, good cholesterol levels and blood pressure – all of these elements add up to a peak-performing cardiovascular health profile.

The U.S. Physicians' Health Study unveiled some of the most dramatic evidence supporting the link between Omega-3-rich fish and heart health. In the study, the eating habits of 20,551 healthy male physicians between the

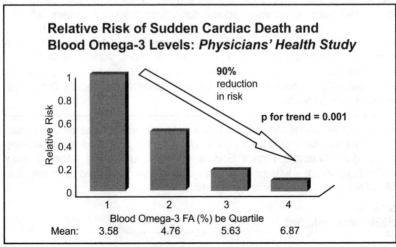

Relative Risk of Sudden Cardiac Death and Blood Omega-3 Levels: *Physicians' Health Study*

90% reduction in risk

p for trend = 0.001

Relative Risk

Blood Omega-3 FA (%) be Quartile

	1	2	3	4
Mean:	3.58	4.76	5.63	6.87

Source: Harris WS. Role of Omega-3 Fatty Acids in Cardiovascular Disease Prevention.
Available at: www.lipidsonline.org/slides/slide01.cfm?tk=42&dpg=6

ages of 40-84 were tracked over 11 years. Physicians who consumed one fish meal per week were found to be associated with a 52% lower risk of sudden cardiac death when compared with physicians who consumed less than one fish meal per month. Researchers concluded that the prospective data suggest that **consuming fish at least once per week may reduce the risk of sudden cardiac death in men.**[48] Further research analyzed the blood levels of Omega-3s EPA and DHA in 15,000 U.S. Physicians' Health Study participants over the course of 17 years. Researchers concluded that **men with the highest levels of Omega-3s in their blood showed a 90% reduction in risk for sudden cardiac death** compared to those with the lowest levels.[49]

Atherosclerosis – a narrowing of the arteries – is among the gravest heart health risk factors. Omega-3s may help keep arteries clear. 162 patients with atherosclerosis were split into two groups – one group was given 6g of fish oil per day for three months, while the other group was given placebo. After three months, the amounts were reduced to 3g per day for an additional 21 months. At study's end, researchers found that twice as many patients in the fish oil group showed a regression in artherosclerotic deposits when compared to the placebo group. **The researchers concluded that fish oil supplementation may be beneficial for atherosclerosis patients.**[50]

Many additional well-designed studies have investigated how Omega-3s impact our cardiovascular system. Among these studies is one that found Omega-3s EPA and DHA make arteries supple and flexible while **reducing pulse pressure and total vascular resistance – effects that researchers believe may reduce the risk of adverse cardiovascular events.**[51] Another research team conducted a study of 43,000 men aged between 40-75, and **discovered that even consuming a small amount of fish (one to three times per month) was associated with a 43% reduction in risk for ischemic stroke.**[52] Yet another study's researchers found that dangerous **arrythmias were significantly reduced for 44% of patients who took fish oil.**[53]

In truth, there are far too many well-designed studies supporting the Omega-3-cardiovascular health link to list in this book. As compelling as this scientific evidence may be, it cannot match the inspiration of true stories from real people whose lives have been profoundly changed by Omega-3s' heart-healthy benefits:

I am a firm believer in Omega-3 fatty acids. My cholesterol was up to 270 total. Then I heard about Omega-3 fatty acids. I gave it a try and my cholesterol dropped by 70 points. I thank God for Omega-3 fatty acids. I feel 10 times better than before – when my cholesterol was high I was tired all of the time. Now I feel great and back to my old self!

Nikki M.
Rocky Mountain, NC

Proper Immune Response

For over 10 years, I have lived with psoriatic arthritis. The simple act of getting out of bed has been sheer torture, and taking care of two small children is sometimes more than I can bear. I have terrible trouble sleeping because lying still for hours causes my body to stiffen, so I wake up every two to three hours so my body won't go into spasms. I have never felt like I was dealing with the root of my problem. My grandmother introduced me to Omega-3 fatty acids. After taking the Omega-3 fatty acids for a week, I noticed the discomfort in my larger joints (hips, shoulders, back) was significantly improving. I feel a boost in my energy, I am thinking more clearly, and I'm finally addressing my discomfort at its core. Omega-3 fatty acids could be the miracle I've been praying for.

Dianne P.
Colorado Springs, CO

When our immune systems are functioning properly, inflammation is our first line of defense – rushing to help us whether we've scraped a knee or we're fighting off an infection. When healing is complete, a well-tuned immune system cools the inflammation back down and waits for the next call to action.

In chronic inflammation, however, the immune system never turns off the inflammation. As a result, the immune system attacks the cells it is supposed to protect, destroying and healing at a voracious pace. This out-of-control assault is increasingly identified as a "silent killer." In fact, integrative medicine specialist Dr. Andrew Weil has proclaimed that "chronic inflammation is a root cause of many serious diseases." The following list represents just a fraction of the conditions associated with chronic inflammation and immune dysfunction:

- Allergy
- Alzheimer's disease
- Arthritis (including rheumatoid)
- Asthma
- Cardiovascular disease
- Chronic fatigue syndrome
- Crohn's disease
- Diabetes (types 1 and 2)
- Fibromyalgia
- Lupus
- Multiple sclerosis
- Obesity

Clearly, when the immune system misfires and inflammation consumes the body like a raging inferno, serious health complications follow. **Thankfully, scientific studies suggest that Omega-3 fatty acids may help to modulate the immune system and inflammatory response.**[54]

Did you know?
In addition to influencing production of the "good" eicosanoids that help to "cool" aggressive inflammation, Omega-3s are believed to modulate inflammation by directly influencing cytokines, which help the immune system communicate, and T cells, a type of "defender" white blood cell.[55]

Let's examine evidence that supports Omega-3s' impact on three of the most prevalent conditions associated with chronic inflammation: Asthma, Rheumatoid Arthritis, and Inflammatory Bowel Disease.

Asthma
Over 20 million Americans and 300 million people worldwide suffer from asthma.[56] It is the most common chronic condition in children. Asthma occurs when "aggressive" eicosanoids activate inflammatory cells, causing airway inflammation, bronchial hyper-responsiveness, bronchospasm, airway edema, and mucus secretion.[57] Anyone who has experienced or witnessed an asthma attack, especially in a child, knows how terrifying they can be. Thankfully, Omega-3s' gentle inflammation-modulating properties appear to hold the potential to help asthma sufferers:

- In one study, fourteen 22-84 year old asthmatics replaced oils in salad dressings and mayonnaise either with oils containing 10-20 grams of corn oil, or with 10-20 grams of Omega-3-rich perilla seed oil. Scientists then recorded forced expiratory volume (FEV1), a common lung function test. After four weeks, a significant improvement in FEV1 was observed in the perilla seed (Omega-3) oil supplementation group – suggesting better lung function. Researchers concluded that perilla seed oil, rich with Omega-3s, may be useful for pulmonary function and in suppressing the inflammatory Leukotrienes associated with asthma.[57]

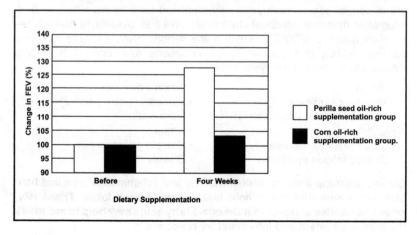

Did you know?
In Tokyo, where the Omega-6 to Omega-3 ratio is 4:1, the childhood asthma rate is only 0.7%[58] – compared to America's estimated 10:1 - 30:1 ratio , where the childhood rate is a whopping 9.4%.[59] Such figures appear to draw a link between Omega-3s' inflammation-modulating activity and asthma.

Rheumatoid Arthritis

Arthritis and Rheumatic conditions are the number one cause of disability in America, affecting 38.4 million people[60]. For arthritis sufferers alone, this number is projected to almost double to 67 million by 2030.[61] Today, an estimated 2.1 million people have rheumatoid arthritis (RA),[62] an auto-immune disease that attacks the linings of the joints. RA is characterized by pain, swelling, stiffness, loss of function, and, at times, fatigue, weight loss, appetite loss, or fever.

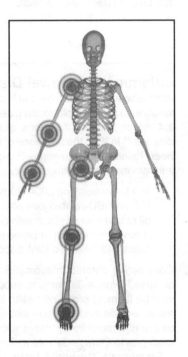

Despite the many research variables, a reduction in the number of tender joints has been one consistent conclusion among studies investigating Omega-3s and RA. Nearly every RA-Omega-3 inter-vention study has found some benefit to fish oil treatment including "reduced duration of morning stiffness, reduced number of tender or swollen joints, reduced joint discomfort, reduced time to fatigue, [and] increased grip strength."[63]

- One 2005 randomized study found that fish oil and olive oil make a good team in promoting joint comfort. In the study, 43 patients took a placebo of soy oil, 3 grams of fish oil, or 3 grams of fish oil and used 9.6 mL of olive oil simply added to salads (providing 6.8 grams of oleic acid), per day. Rheumatoid Arthritis (RA) symptoms were measured at 12 weeks and 24 weeks of treatment. At study's end, compared to placebo, both the fish oil and fish/olive oil groups enjoyed an improvement in joint discomfort intensity, right and left handgrip strength, duration of morning stiffness, onset of fatigue, ability to bend down to pick up clothing from the floor, and getting in and out of a car. **The researchers concluded that fish oil produced beneficial effects and reduced clinical symptoms of RA, while the fish and olive oil group showed even more beneficial effects.**[64]

I'm a young 54-year-old woman, very active and very healthy. A few years ago the discs in my lower spine started grinding so loudly that it became embarrassing. Whenever I turned or sat down or got up the bones would grind. I had read an article somewhere about how Omega-3s help support joints, and thought I'd give it a try. Well! It took care of the joint discomfort I had! I was ecstatic!

**Lynda C.
Portland, ME**

Inflammatory Bowel Disease

After Rheumatoid Arthritis, the most common chronic inflammatory condition in America is the autoimmune disease Inflammatory Bowel Disease (IBD) with 1.4 million suffering from one of its two forms, Ulcerative Colitis or Crohn's disease.[65] In IBD, the presence of high levels of inflammatory eicosanoids has been found in the intestines.[66] Scientific evidence suggests that Omega-3s' inflammation-modulating activity might help IBD sufferers.

- In a two-week long 2004 study, researchers found that for 38 patients with IBD and IBD-related joint pain, consuming 6.5 grams of Omega-3 rich seal oil or cod liver oil (each with between 2.3 and 3.7 of EPA/DHA), both "had a tendency toward improvement of IBD disease activity," in addition to helping IBD-related joint discomfort.[67]

Considering chronic inflammation's devastating potential as "the root of all disease," Omega-3s' immune-supporting and inflammation-modulating activity may be its most profound health benefit of all. In the preceding three studies alone, we see evidence suggesting that Omega-3s' role in immunity may help us breathe more freely, move with ease and digest nutritious foods – adding credence to Omega-3s' role as important "survival" nutrients for humanity.

Simply put, **Omega-3 fatty acids promote immune system health.** With a peak-performing immune system, our bodies respond with a balanced defense to threats; signaling for aggressive inflammation when needed and cooling that inflammation when the danger has passed. As Omega-3s work to harmonize the immune system's performance, they take on yet another crucial role in supporting our overall well-being: helping to protect us and heal us.

As much Omega-3 territory as we've covered to this point, there are still many stones left unturned. Read on to hear about Omega-3s' ever-expanding range of surprising potential health benefits.

Health Benefits
You Never Imagined

"Omega-3s have dramatically improved my health!"

I started taking Omega-3s when I got the results of my blood sugar and cholesterol tests – they were too high. I was also experiencing shortness of breath, fatigue, hot flashes, and excessively dry skin. Omega-3s have dramatically improved my health! My sugar level has been reduced from 116 to 93, my triglyceride levels have lowered, and my high density lipo-protein (HDL) [good cholesterol] has increased. Additionally, my hair growth and luster have improved, and my skin is much smoother. I feel more alert mentally and physically, and I have experienced better digestion. I have almost forgotten what hot flashes are; they are less frequent and last only for a very short time. I also feel that Omega-3s serve as a lubricant to my joints, just like motor oil for a vehicle.

Theresa A.
Portland, OR

"Life is now great for me, and my thanks go to Omega-3s."

I started taking Omega-3s when I was 68 years old and suffering terribly from arthritis. Upon waking every morning, I could not walk without discomfort bringing tears to my eyes. After three months of taking Omega-3s, what a relief! I can now walk two miles daily, swim, ride my bicycle and even play with my five-year-old grand-daughter. Believe it or not, Omega-3s also helped me with my constipation. I have also noticed that my skin feels so much softer and smoother. What a difference Omega-3s have made in my life! To my delight, they have made me feel much younger. I highly recommend that everyone take Omega-3s – they will change your life for the better and give you energy you didn't know you had. Life is now great for me, and my thanks go to Omega-3s.

Nancy V.
Houston, TX

A SIMPLE, ANCIENT SOLUTION TO MODERN HEALTH PROBLEMS

Four thousand years ago, Egyptians ordered the digging of a canal connecting Europe to Asia through the Mediterranean Sea, Red Sea, and the Nile River. Ancients used this Suez Canal to trade the Omega-3-rich flax that grew on the banks of Nile and harvest fish that would later become a staple in the famous Mediterranean diet. Today, cultures that subsist on this Omega-3-rich diet are known for their vitality, longevity, and reduced incidence of the chronic diseases that plague modern America.

Start moving towards a nutritious, whole food diet aimed at achieving the life our bodies were made for and put trust in nature's plan: our children and loved ones will be there to thank us with healthy bodies and minds. The key to reversing the startling increase in modern health problems may be locked in the history of ancient diets focused on high Omega-3 intake.

SWIFT FISH REST ASSURED: WEIGHT LOSS

As humans register unprecedented rates of weight gains, the singular solution for weight loss remains unknown. Many factors will be involved in helping you and those you love to lose weight. Exploring a healthy Omega-3 ratio for your body should be one of them.

- In one study designed to test the effect of various fish oil dosages on resting metabolic rate (a weight management factor), 32 healthy men and women ingested safflower oil or varying dosages of fish oil for 28 days. The study indicated that those taking 1.5 grams of Omega-3s (in fish oil) daily had the highest increase in resting metabolic rate. Further, for all except the safflower group, triglycerides – one of the many culprits implicated in the metabolic syndrome that accompanies obesity – were reduced.[68]

For the past two summers, I have volunteered at the Grand Portage National Monument on the shores of Lake Superior. When I started I weighed about 315 pounds, had hypertension and suffered from pulmonary edema. I couldn't walk a block without gasping for breath. During each of those summers I lost an average of 20 pounds. As the pounds disappeared, I noticed that I could walk longer and faster. I wondered why. This past summer I read a study conducted in Australia which showed people who exercised and took Omega-3 fish oil lost an amazing amount of weight. I looked at my summer diet and realized that I was eating Lake Superior herring three times a week. I had been taking Omega-3 supplements, but never in large quantities. I decided to give this experiment a try and increase my Omega-3 intake. Today I have lost an additional 10 pounds; down to 265. My hypertension is under control and I have not suffered any pulmonary edema. I have more weight to lose, but I'm confident that with exercise and Omega-3s' help, I will achieve my goals.

John K.
San Antonio, TX

SWIMMINGLY STRONG: BONE HEALTH

For many people, bone health and the prevention of osteoporosis should be the focus of a proper nutrition, supplementation and exercise regimen for at least half a lifetime. The National Institute of Arthritis and Musculoskeletal and Skin Diseases states: "One out of every two women and one in four men over 50 will have an osteoporosis-related fracture in their lifetime."[69] While building critical bone mass begins at year one, studies show that bone-building rates increase drastically with age for both men and women.[71]

Research suggests that Omega-3s may help our bones stay strong at critical development phases. One Swedish 1994 study of 78 healthy young male volunteers (illustrated in the chart at right) found that, at 22 years of age, higher DHA blood levels correlated with increased spine and total body bone mineral density.[71] The study's authors invite more research to validate their conclusions: that Omega-3s are associated with bone density gains.

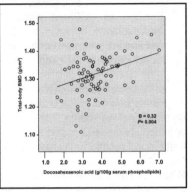

SEA YOUR WAY TO EYE HEALTH

Age-related macular degeneration (AMD) threatens to decimate quality of life by impairing vision and causing blindness. To investigate Omega-3s' impact on AMD, Harvard Medical School and other researchers analyzed food intakes of over 72,000 male and female nurses and doctors, age 50+, none of whom had AMD. At study's end, researchers concluded that those who ate more than four servings of fish per week had 35% less development of AMD than those who ate three servings or less fish per month. The research suggests links between DHA intake, fish intake and protection from AMD.[72]

I am 67 years old. In 2006, I was diagnosed with AMD, the leading cause of blindness in the older population. The Casey Eye Clinic in Portland is a nationally recognized leader in eye care and research. They, along with the National Eye Institute (NEI), suggested after extensive research that Omega-3s play a significant role in slowing the progression of AMD. I take 1,200 mg of Omega-3s daily, and in the last two months, my eyesight has actually slightly improved, which is very reassuring. With Omega-3s and the Casey Eye Clinic, my eyesight future looks bright.

William M.
Portland, OR

SCALES ARE FOR FISH: SKIN HEALTH

Diseases of the skin such as eczema are increasingly prevalent in the modern world; 15 million Americans suffer from atopic eczema.[73] Researchers continue to investigate the long-held belief that the reduced consumption of Omega-3 oils in the Western Diet is linked to the rise of eczema.

- 44 eczema sufferers, ages 18-40, were tracked over the course of eight weeks while taking over five grams of DHA and a small amount of EPA or a similar amount of caprylic and capric acid. At study's end DHA groups showed an 18% improvement, while control groups showed an 11% improvement; however, for DHA groups the number of affected areas decreased, whereas control groups showed no change. The researchers concluded that DHA can act as an aid to standard eczema treatment.[74]

Given that eczema almost always begins in childhood, it's easy to see how this frustrating skin condition could have a significant and lasting negative impact on emotional well-being. The millions of eczema sufferers may find cause for optimism, however, reading success stories like the following – which suggest that natural nutrition may help give them control over the misery of eczema:

When my son was 18 months old I found a small patch of eczema on his leg. As he got older, more spots of eczema surfaced, especially behind his knees and in the insides of his elbows. We put creams on him that seemed to help a little, but nothing took away the eczema. He itched a lot, especially at night. The eczema was so bad that baths and showers caused him a lot of pain – he hated them! All the doctors could offer were steroids. I knew that God could not create children to have skin conditions like this, and I prayed that he could show us the answer. One day I talked to a friend who suggested that we try [the Omega-3 fatty acid] EPA. My son began to take two capsules with every meal. Within 10 days his eczema was almost gone.

Linda M.
Pottsville, PA

DON'T FLOUNDER AROUND WITH PMS

Earlier we discussed how Omega-3s can benefit pregnancy and infants. But can they also help the millions of women who are preparing for these life stages, as well as women who continue to work and support families within their childbearing years? Premenstrual syndrome can derail these women with a collection of symptoms that can be severe enough to interfere with day-to-day life. Evidence suggests that Omega-3s may gain nutritional favor with women worldwide by offering some relief from PMS's frustrating symptoms.

- One study compared the effects of various oils mixtures on menstrual discomfort for 70 Danish women, ages 16-49. Women were divided into placebo oil, seal oil, fish oil, or fish oil with B12 supplemented groups. Over three months, symptoms of menstrual discomfort were reduced in all the

Omega-3-rich oil groups, with the fish oil with B12 group enjoying the most relief. Researchers concluded that a combination of Omega-3s and B12 might aid in menstrual discomfort.[75]

PONDER THIS: MIGRAINES

Throbbing pain, nausea, sensitivity to light and sound – when migraines strike, sufferers retreat to a quiet, dark room to lie down and wait for the agony to subside. Distressingly, America saw an increase of 60% in the number of migraine sufferers throughout the 1980s with almost 71% of this increase occurring in those younger than age 45.[76] Migraine sufferers who are compelled to explore any and all options that may help alleviate their attacks might be intrigued by the following Omega-3 fatty acid study:

- 27 adolescents with chronic migraines took two grams of either fish oil or olive oil for two months, abstained from supplementation for one month, and then switched to the opposite oil. In all supplementation groups, headache frequency, duration, and severity were reduced. Researchers suggest that the positive results of both oils indicate a response beyond "the placebo effect," and that both should be further tested as a beneficial treatment in migraine relief.[77]

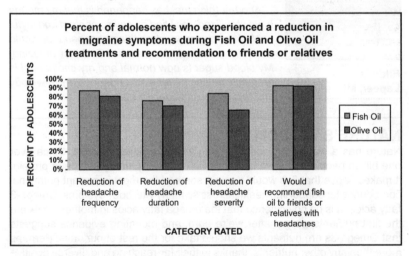

Percent of adolescents who experienced a reduction in migraine symptoms during Fish Oil and Olive Oil treatments and recommendation to friends or relatives

Omega-3s' nutritional support for heart health and pregnancy is well-known, but who knew these nutrients were associated with so many other areas of wellness? Researchers continue to investigate Omega-3s' far-reaching impact on human health, so more pleasant surprises may be in store. As Omega-3s help to promote well-being within our bodies' very cells, health benefits appear to expand and multiply, culminating in an amazing revelation: Many who focus on Omega-3 intake start to feel great about themselves, every single day.

Nature's Gift for Vibrant Life

My story began the summer of 2007 when my lab results came back with high cholesterol and blood sugar. I changed my diet to no sugar and no white carbs. I looked up glycemic levels for veggies and fruits and ate the low-level ones often. I also cut down on meat and added lots of fiber to my diet.

I began using the Omega-3 fish oil at this time to help with my cholesterol levels. After an initial weight loss of 5 pounds, I hit a plateau and felt discour-

aged – but I continued on my new way of eating and using supplements, hoping to help my blood sugar and cholesterol. By the end of summer I had lost 21 pounds. I credit Omega-3s for kicking in my metabolism to boost my weight loss.

Another thing that has happened is that my moods have stabilized and I find myself so content and joyful each day now, even when things happen that would normally make me depressed. I find that amazing. My blood sugar is now normal and my cholesterol is gradually getting better also. I now love my new body and this new emotional life I am living.

Ellen D.
Lapeer, MI

NATURE'S WISDOM

Nature has a way of providing us with what we need to thrive. Since over one billion people in the world rely on fish as their primary source of protein, it makes sense that fish would contain some of the most important nutritional compounds for supporting health across so many vital body systems: Omega-3 fatty acids. It is no coincidence that the omega fatty acids in mother's milk are the first nutrients we get after we're born, and mounting evidence suggests that Omega-3s are nutrients we should take for the rest of our days. Perhaps more than any other nutrients, thanks to their far-reaching and diverse positive impact on human health, Omega-3s hold the potential to change the world.

Can you imagine if the health of nearly 400 million people could be enhanced by Omega-3s? What a beautiful life we could build for the 133.6 million overweight Americans,[78] the 15 million eczema sufferers,[79] the 43.6 million over-age-50 at risk for osteoporosis of the hip alone,[80] the 40.8 million PMS sufferers,[81] and the 32 million adult migraine sufferers.[82] Visualize the quality of life improvements we could promote for 24 million Americans with diagnosed heart disease,[83] 20 million asthma sufferers,[84] 38 million arthritis sufferers,[85] and 1.5 million people struggling with IBD.[86] Finally, think of the mental clarity and peace of mind we could bring to 47 million people with mood problems[87] and 24 million with age-related memory impairment.[88]

These goals are within reach – and since they only recap the areas of health discussed in this brief introductory book, they may just be the tip of the iceberg in terms of Omega-3s' potential health benefits.

LOVING LIFE

Whether the studies featured in this book help you to imagine a different world where health flows into your life like a refreshing river or whether you begin to think more carefully about the health of those you love, the end conclusion is the same: Omega-3s deserve a part in the adventure of life. And, when you eliminate chronic nagging conditions and possess crystal clear thinking, flexible joints, keen eyesight, a strong heart and healthy weight, that is what life becomes: an exhilarating adventure.

Throughout the true stories featured in this book, Omega-3s are hailed as helping with various health conditions. But perhaps most intriguing are the more esoteric themes these powerful testimonials present: stories of happiness, joy, energy, optimism and passion for living. For many of those who shared their stories in this book, Omega-3s are identified as the key to this elevated quality of life.

It makes sense: if a nutrient starts by supporting your cells, then expands to positively impact health on many different levels – why shouldn't we start feeling better, with zest and enthusiasm for each dawning day? Abundant and ever-increasing research suggests Omega-3s may be doing just that.

Enhance your diet with the right fats, and you may find yourself sharing those exhilarating feelings of whole-life happiness. The solution to true vibrant life may be as simple as investing in an enduring, powerful health icon that's been present from ancient history to modern science: Omega-3 fatty acids.

OMEGA-3 LIFESTYLE CHECKLIST
Expert Insight
☑ Before you start increasing your Omega-3 intake, be sure to consult with a qualified healthcare professional. Start with your family doctor, but keep an open mind about nutritionists, dieticians, and other practitioners. It is important to take the exact amount of Omega-3 suggested by your health practitioner.

Diet
☑ Balance your ratio: Experts believe that balancing the ratio of Omega-6 to Omega-3 diets may be a key to achieving true well-being. To bring your ratio into balance, reduce intake of Omega-6 foods and increase intake of Omega-3 foods. In simple terms: eat a healthier diet. Omega-6 fatty acids are usually abundant in the "junk" foods we know we should avoid; things like fried foods, processed foods, excessive grain-fed red meat, and trans-fats. Omega-6s are also often present in breads, cereals, and grain-fed cheese and dairy

products. Omega-3s, on the other hand, are not surprisingly found in many of the foods that are defining the natural health movement: soybeans, flaxseed, chia seed, grass-fed meat and dairy, olive oil, and leafy green vegetables.

Fish Intake

☑ Of course, don't forget the most famous source of Omega-3s: fish. The following fish include some of the best for Omega-3 intake:

- Tuna
- Salmon
- Mackerel
- Herring
- Trout

- Sardines
- Halibut
- Oysters
- Shrimp
- Scallops

Buy wild fish whenever possible; farmed fish may contain lower levels of Omega-3s. Unfortunately, mercury risk in many Omega-3-rich fish (most notably in tuna and mackerel) makes it harder to eat enough to gain Omega-3 health benefits.

Omega-3 Supplements:

Getting Omega-3 in supplement form holds several advantages over getting Omega-3 from dietary changes alone:

Consistency

If you order a piece of salmon at a restaurant, you can be certain you'll be getting some Omega-3s... the mystery is, how much? It's an impossible question – Omega-3 levels can vary dramatically, even within the same species of fish. Quality supplements have the advantage of delivering the same precise level of Omega-3s every time, so you know exactly what you're getting.

Safety

Top quality Omega-3 supplements undergo rigorous testing to prove that they are not only fresh, pure, and potent, but also mercury-free and PCB-free.

Affordability

Eating fish a couple of times a week can be prohibitively expensive. Supplements offer all the health-promoting benefits of Omega-3s (plus consistency and safety) without the expense of eating fish.

Convenience

Not everybody's Julia Child. It takes some skill in the kitchen to choose fresh fish and prepare it into a delicious meal. Supplements deliver Omega-3s without the hassle of buying fish, cooking it and cleaning up afterwards.

1. Rudin D, Felix C. Omega-3 Oils, a Practical Guide. Avery, 1996.

2. Allport S. The Queen of Fats: Why Omega-3s Were Removed from the Western Diet and What We Can Do to Replace them. Berkeley University of California Press, 2006.

3. Kang J. The Importance of Omega-6/Omega-3 Fatty Acid Ratio in Cell Function. Simopoulos AP, Cleland LG (eds): Omega-6/Omega-3 Essential Fatty Acid Ratio: The Scientific Evidence. World Rev Nutr Diet. Basel, Karger, 2003, vol 92, pp 23-36.

4. Teale, MC, Bienkiewicz G, Calder PC. Omega 3 Fatty Acid Research. Nova Publishers, 2006.

5. National Institutes of Health, Office of Dietary Supplements. Omega-3 Fatty Acids and Health. Available at: http://ods.od.nih.gov/FactSheets/Omega3FattyAcidsandHealth.asp.

6. Zurier RB. Fatty Acids, Inflammation and Immune Responses. Prostaglandins, Leukotrienes and Essential Fatty Acids. (1993) 48. 57-62.

7. Simopoulos, A. Omega 3 fatty acids in wild plants, nuts and seeds. Asia Pacific J Clin Nutr (2002) 11(S6) S163-S173.

8. Journal of Clinical Nutrition 83 (6, supplement): 1505S–1519S. American Society for Nutrition. PMID 16841861.

9. Stoll A. The Omega-3 Connection. Simon and Shuster, 2001.

10. U. S. Department of Health and Human Services, U.S. Environmental Protection Agency. What You Need to Know About Mercury in Fish and Shellfish. 2004. Available at: http://www.cfsan.fda.gov/~dms/admehg3.html.

11. National Health and Nutrition Examination III. Available at: http://www.cdc.gov/nchs/products/elec_prods/subject/nhanes3.htm.

12. University of Maryland Medical Center: Omega Fatty Acids. Available at: http://www.umm.edu/altmed/articles/omega-3-000316.htm.

13. The World's Healthiest Foods. Available at: http://www.whfoods.com/genpage.php?tname=nutrient&dbid=84., the following symptoms are associated with Omega-3 deficiency.

14. Walker M. Pregnancy Requires Omega-3 EFAs. Health Foods Business, Sept. 1995, Pages 39, 85.

15. Jacobson J, Jacobson S, Muckle G, Kaplan-Estrin M, Ayotte P, Dewailly E. Beneficial Effects of a Polyunsaturated Fatty Acid on Infant Development: Evidence from the Inuit of Artic Quebec. The Journal of Pediatrics Volume 152, Issue 3, Pages 356-364.e1 (March 2008).

16. Jensen C. Effects of n-3 fatty acids during pregnancy and lactation. American Journal of Clinical Nutrition, Vol. 83, No. 6, S1452-1457S, June 2006.

17. Olson SF, Secher NJ. Low consumption of seafood in early pregnancy as a risk factor for preterm delivery: prospective cohort study. British Medical Journal, Vol. 324 (7335), Feb. 23, 2002.

18. Williams A, et al. Omega-3 Fatty Acids in Maternal Erythrocytes and Risk of Preeclampsia, Epidemiology, Vol. 6, No. 3 (May 1995), pp. 232-237.

19. Holman R, et al. Deficiency of essential fatty acids and membrane fluidity during pregnancy and lactation. Proc. Natl. Acad. Sci. USA. Vol 88, pp 4835-4839, June 1991.

20. Hibbeln, JR. Long-chain polyunsaturated fatty acids in depression and related conditions, Phospholipid Spectrum Disorder, M. Peet, I. Glen, and D. Horrobin, eds. Lancshire, England: Marius Press, 1999, 195-210.

21. Matsudaira T. Attention deficit disorders--drugs or nutrition? Nutr Health. 2007;19(1-2):57-60.

22. Connor K, SanGiovanni JP, Lofqvist C, Maderman C, Chen J, et al. Increased dietary intake of omega-3-polyunsaturated fatty acids reduces pathological retinal angiogenesis. Nature Medicine, 13, 868–873, July 1, 2007.

23. Singh, M. Essential fatty acids, DHA and human brain, Indian Journal of Pediatrics, 2005; Vol.72, Issue 3, pp. 239-242.

24. Helleland IB, Smith L, Saarem K, Saugstad D, Drevon CA. Maternal supplementation with very long chain n-3 fatty acids during pregnancy and lactation augments children's IQ at 4 years of age. Pediatrics 111 (1):e39-e44, 2003.

25. Stevens L, Zentall S, Abate M, et al. Omega-3 fatty acids in boys with behavior, learning, and health problems. Physiol Behav, 1996; 59 (4-5): 915-920.

26. Whalley L, Fox HC, Wahle K, Starr JM, Deary I, Cognitive aging, childhood intelligence, and the use of food supplements: possible involvement of n-3 fatty acids, American Journal of Clinical Nutrition 2004; 80: 1650-7.

27. University of Pittsburgh Medical Center (2006, March 4). Omega 3 Fatty Acids Influence Mood, Impulsivity And Personality, Study Indicates. ScienceDaily.

28. Sobczak S, Honig A, Christophe A, et al. Lower high-density lipoprotein cholesterol and increased omega-6 polyunsaturated fatty acids in first-degree relatives of bipolar patients. Psychol Med. 2004;34(1):103-12.

29. Fontani G, Corradeschi F, Felici A, Alfatti F, Migliorini S, Lodi L. Cognitive and physiological effects of Omega-3 polyunsaturated fatty acid supplementation in healthy subjects.European Journal of Clinical Investigation. 2005 Nov; 35 (11): 691-9.

30. Kalmijn S, van Boxtel MPJ, Ocke M, et al. Dietary intake of fatty acids and fish in relation to cognitive performance at middle age. Neurol 2004; 62: 275-280.

31. [Ma Q, Teter B, Ubeda O, et al. Omega-3 fatty acid docosahexaenoic acid increases SorLA/LR11, a sorting protein with reduced expression in sporadic Alzheimer's disease (AD): relevance to AD prevention. J Neurosci. 2007; 27 (52): 14299-307.

32. Barberger-Gateau P, Letenneur L, et al. Fish, meat, and risk of dementia: cohort study. British Medical Journal 2002; 325: 932-933.

33. Kung, HC et al. Deaths: Final Data for 2005. Volume 56, Number 10. April 24, 2008. National Vital Statistics Reports.

34. World Health Organization. World Health Statistics 2008 Report. Available at: http://www.who.int/whosis/whostat/2008/en/index.html

35. Kris-Etherton P, Harris W, Appel L. Fish Consumption, Fish Oil, Omega-3 Fatty Acids, and Cardiovascular Disease. Circulation 2002;106;2747-2757

36. Lupton, J. U.S. National Academy of Sciences website; "Dietary Reference Intakes For Energy, Carbohydrate, Fiber, Fat, Fatty Acids, Cholesterol, Protein, and Amino Acids."

37. Available at: www.fda.gov/bbs/topics/news/2004/NEW01115.html.

38. Department of Health and Human Services. Report of the Dietary Guidelines Advisory Committee on the Dietary Guidelines for Americans, 2005. August 19, 2004. Available at: http://www.health.gov/dietaryguidelines/dga2005/report.

39. Kang JX, Leaf A. Antiarrhythmic effects of polyunsaturated fatty acids. Circulation 1996;94:1774–80.

40. Simopoulos AP. Omega-3 Fatty Acids in Inflammation and Autoimmune Diseases. Journal of the American College of Nutrition, 2002 21(6): 495–505.

41. Goode GK, Garcia S, Heagerty AM. Dietary supplementation with marine fish oil improves in vitro small artery endothelial function in hypercholesterolemic patients: a double-blind placebo-controlled study. Circulation. 1997;96:2802–2807.

42. Nestel P, et al. The n-3 fatty acids eicosapentaenoic acid and docosahexaenoic acid increase systemic arterial compliance in humans. Am J Clin Nutr, 76, 2:326-30, 2002.

43. Khan F, et al, The effects of dietary fatty acid supplementation on endothelial function and vascular tone in healthy subjects. Cardiovascular Research 59 (2003), 955-962.

44. Simopoulos AP. Omega-3 Fatty Acids in Inflammation and Autoimmune Diseases. Journal of the American College of Nutrition, 2002 21(6): 495–505.

45. Harris WS, et al. Cardiovascular disease and long chain omega-3 fatty acids. Curr Opin Lipidol. 2003 Feb;14(1):9-14.

46. Ueshima H, Stamler J, Elliott P, Chan Q, Brown IJ, Carnethon MR, Daviglus ML, He K, Moag-Stahlberg A, Rodriguez BL, Steffen LM, Van Horn L, Yarnell J, Zhou B. Food Omega-3 Fatty Acid Intake of Individuals (Total, Linolenic Acid, Long-Chain) and Their Blood Pressure. INTERMAP Study. Hypertension. 2007 Jun 4; [Epub ahead of print . PMID:17548718.

47. Bonaa KH, Bjerve KS, Straume B, Gram IT, Thelle D. Effect of eicosapentaenoic and docosahexaenoic acids on blood pressure in hypertension. A population-based intervention trial from the Tromso study. N. Engl. J. Med. 1990; 322: 795–801.

48. Albert CM, Hennekens CH, O'Donnell CJ, Ajani UA, Carey VJ. Fish consumption and risk of sudden cardiac death. JAMA 1998;279:23–7.

References

49. Albert CM, Campos H, Stampfer MJ, et al. Blood levels of long-chain n-3 fatty acids and the risk of sudden death. N Engl J Med 2002;346:1113-1118.

50. von Schacky, Clemens, et al. The effect of dietary omega-3 fatty acids on coronary atherosclerosis. Annals of Internal Medicine, 1999;130: 554-562.

51. Nestel P et al. The n-fatty acids eicosapentaenoic acid and docosahexaenoic acid increase systemic arterial compliance in humans. Am J Clin Nutr, 76, 2:326-30, 2002.

52. He K, Rimm E, Merchant A, et al. Fish consumption and risk of stroke in men. The Journal of the American Medical Association 2002; 288: 3130-3136.

53. Sellmayer A, Witzgall H, Lorez RL, Weber PC. Effects of dietary fish oil on ventricular premature complexes. Am J Cardiol. 1995; 76:974.

54. Simopoulos AP. Omega-3 Fatty Acids in Inflammation and Autoimmune Diseases. Journal of the American College of Nutrition, 2002 21(6): 495–505.

55. Zurier, RB. Fatty Acids, Inflammation and Immune Response. Prostaglandins, Leukotrienes and Essential Fatty Acids (1993) 48. 57-62.

56. Mickleborough TD, Rundell KW. Dietary polyunsaturated fatty acids in asthma- and exercise-induced bronchoconstriction. European Journal of Clinical Nutrition, 2005 59: 1335–1346.

57. Okamoto M, Mitsunobu F, Ashida K, Mifune T, Hosaki Y, Tsugeno H, Harada S, Tanizaki Y. Effects of n-3 fatty acids on asthma. Internal Medicine, 2000 Feb 39(2).

58. Omega-3s and childhood asthma. (Letters to the Editor). Thorax, 2002 Mar 57(3): 281.

59. Centers for Disease Control, FASTATS Asthma. Available at: http://www.cdc.gov/nchs/FASTATS/asthma.htm.

60. United States Department of Health and Human Services (US), Centers for Disease Control and Prevention. Direct and Indirect Costs of Arthritis and Other Rheumatic Conditions -- United States, 1997 [Internet]. Available at http://www.cdc.gov/mmwr/preview/mmwrhtml/mm5246a3.htm.

61. Hootman JM, Helmick CG. Arthritis Rheum. Projections of US prevalence of arthritis and associated activity limitations. 2006 Jan;54(1):226-9.

62. National Institutes of Health (US), National Center for Complementary and Alternative Medicine. Rheumatoid Arthritis and Complementary and Alternative Medicine. Bethesda (MD): The Institute; 2005 Sept.

63. Calder PC. n–3 Polyunsaturated fatty acids, inflammation, and inflammatory diseases. American Journal of Clinical Nutrition, 2006 Jun 83(6): S1505-1519S.

64. Berbert AA, Kondo CR, Almendra CL, Matsuo T, Dichi I. Supplementation of fish oil and olive oil in patients with rheumatoid arthritis. Nutrition, 2005 21:131–6.

65. Loftus EV Jr. Clinical Epidemiology of Inflammatory Bowel Disease: Incidence, Prevalence, and Environmental Influences. Gastroenterology, 2004 126:1504–1517.

66. Calder PC. n–3 Polyunsaturated fatty acids, inflammation, and inflammatory diseases. American Journal of Clinical Nutrition, 2006 Jun 83(6): S1505-1519S.

67. Brunborg LA, Madland TM, Lind RA, Arslan G, Berstad A, Frøyland L. Effects of short-term oral administration of dietary marine oils in patients with inflammatory bowel disease and joint pain: A pilot study comparing seal oil and cod liver oil. Clinical Nutrition, 2008, doi:10.1016/j.clnu.2008.01.017.

68. Noreen EE, Petrella RJ, Lemon PWR. Effects of varying doses of fish oil supplementation on resting metabolic rate and body composition. Medicine & Science in Sports & Exercise, May 2003 35(5): S248.

69. National Institutes of Health (US), National Institute of Arthritis and Musculoskeletal and Skin Diseases. Osteoporosis modified 2007 Dec. Available from: http://www.niams.nih.gov/Health_Info/Bone/Osteoporosis/default.asp.

70. U.S. Department of Health and Human Services. Bone health and osteoporosis: A report of the Surgeon General. Rockville, MD: U.S. Department of Health and Human Services, Office of the Surgeon General, 2004.

71. Högstrom M, Nordström P, Nordström A. n-3 Fatty acids are positively associated with peak bone mineral density and bone accrual in healthy men: the NO2 Study1-3. Amer Journ of Clin Nutr, 2007 85: 803-7.

72. Cho E, Hung S, Willett WC, Spiegelman D, Rimm EB, Seddon JM, Colditz GA, Hankinson SE. Prospective study of dietary fat and the risk of age-related macular degeneration. American Journal of Clinical Nutrition, Feb 2001 73(2): 209-218.

73. National Institutes of Health (US), National Institute of Arthritis and Musculoskeletal and Skin Diseases. Atopic dermatitis [Internet.] Bethesda (MD): The Institute; 1999 Jan [modified 2003 Apr; cited 2008 May 8.] Available: www.niams.nih.gov/Health_Info/Atopic/default.asp]

74. Koch C, Dölle S, Metzger M, Rasche C, Jungclas H, Rühl R, Renz H, Worm, M. Docosahexaenoic acid (DHA) supplementation in atopic eczema: a randomized, double-blind, controlled trial. British Journal of Dermatology, Apr 2008 158(4): 786-792.

75. Deutch B, Jørgensen EB, Hansen JC. Menstrual discomfort in Danish women reduced by dietary supplements of omega-3 PUFA and B12 (fish oil or seal oil capsules). Nutrition Research, 2000 20(5): 621-631.

76. (US), Centers for Disease Control and Prevention. Current trends prevalence of chronic migraine headaches --- United States, 1980 - 1989 [Internet.] Atlanta, GA: United States Department of Health and Human Services, Centers for Disease Control and Prevention; [html conversion 1998 Aug 5; cited 2008 May 12.] (Morbidity and Mortality Weekly Report). Available from: http://www.cdc.gov/mmwr/preview/mmwrhtml/00001982.htm.

77. Harel Z, Gascon G, Riggs S, Vaz R, Brown W, Exil G. Supplementation with omega-3 polyunsaturated fatty acids in the management of recurrent migraines in adolescents. Journal of Adolescent Health, Aug 2002 31(2): 154-61.

78. National Institutes of Health (US), National Institute of Diabetes and Digestive and Kidney Diseases (NIDDK), Weight-control Information Network (WIN). Statistics related to overweight and obesity [Internet.] Rockville, MD: The Institute; [modified 2007 Jun; cited 2008 May 12.] Available from: http://win.niddk.nih.gov/statistics/index.htm.

79. National Institutes of Health (US), National Institute of Arthritis and Musculoskeletal and Skin Diseases. Atopic dermatitis [Internet.] Bethesda (MD): The Institute; 1999 Jan [modified 2003 Apr; cited 2008 May 8.] Available from: http://www.niams.nih.gov/Health_Info/Atopic_Dermatitis/default.asp

80. U.S. Department of Health and Human Services. Bone health and osteoporosis: A report of the Surgeon General. Rockville, MD: U.S. Department of Health and Human Services, Office of the Surgeon General, 2004.

81. United States Department of Health and Human Services (US), The National Women's Health Information Center, Office on Women's Health. Premenstrual syndrome [Internet.] Rockville, MD: United States Department of Health and Human Services (US), The National Women's Health Information Center, Office on Women's Health; 2007 Jan [cited 2008 May 11]. Available from: http://www.womenshealth.gov/faq/pms.htm.

82. U.S. National Center for Health Statistics. Table 190. Persons 18 years of age and over with migraines and pains in the neck, lower back, face or jaw, by selected characteristics: 2005 [Internet.] [cited 2008 May 12.] Available from: http://www.census.gov/compendia/statab/tables/08s0190.pdf.

83. US. Dept. of Health and Human Services. Centers for Disease Control and Prevention. Summary Health Statistics for U.S. Adults: National Health Interview Survey, 2006. DHHS Publication No. (PHS) 2008-1563.

84. US. Dept. of Health and Human Services. Centers for Disease Control and Prevention. Summary Health Statistics for U.S. Adults: National Health Interview Survey, 2006, Tables 3 and 4; Table 1, Appendix III, Table IV. DHHS Publication No. (PHS) 2008-1563.

85. US. Dept. of Health and Human Services. Centers for Disease Control and Prevention. Summary Health Statistics for U.S. Adults: National Health Interview Survey, 2006, Tables 7 and 8. DHHS Publication No. (PHS) 2008-1563.

86. US. Dept. of Health and Human Services. Centers for Disease Control and Prevention. Division of Adult and Community Health. Inflammatory Bowel Disease. Available at: www.cdc.gov/nccdphp/dach/ibd.htm

87. National Institute of Mental Health. The Numbers Count: Mental Disorders in America. Available at: http://www.nimh.nih.gov/health/publications/the-numbers-count-mental-disorders-in-america.shtml

88. Ferri et al (2005) Global prevalence of dementia: a Delphi consensus study. The Lancet 366, 2112-2117.